TONGUE TO THE ANVIL

New and selected poems

Thomas Alan Orr

RESTORATION
PRESS

Restoration Press
1035 Hosbrook Street
Indianapolis, Indiana 46203 USA

General Editor: Tim J. Harmon / timjharmon@gmail.com
Design and Layout: Janet Fry Schneider

First Edition
ISBN 978-0-9821840-5-9

The author wishes to thank Dan Carpenter and Mark Alan
Goodman for reading early drafts of this book and offering
their advice and wisdom. Whatever faults remain are entirely
his own.

Cover: The author's grandfather, George Willard Orr, and
team cultivating potatoes, East Bangor, Maine, c. 1925

Grateful acknowledgement is made to the publications in
which some of these poems first appeared: Tipton Poetry
Review, Merton Seasonal, Flying Island, Hopewell Review

"Farm Hands" and "Circling Square" are included by
permission of Brick Street Poetry, Inc.

"Letter from Camp Morton" and "Tongue Wagging" were
originally composed for "shadow box" art presentations created
by Tim Harmon and first displayed at the Harrison Gallery in
Indianapolis.

Printed in the United States of America

For Tess

In better dress to trim thee was my mind,
But naught save homespun cloth in the house I find.

– Anne Bradstreet
"The Author to Her Book" (1678)

Contents

The Conversion of Dewey Lomax

Afterward he lay three days on a cot in the back room
Of Brother Braddock's place out by Little Blue River,
Croaking dark prophesies between bouts of fever.

Tiger lilies blazed like tongues of fire
On the brow of the land rising up from Little Blue,
Where herons bowed in the high sycamores.

Nobody in the Holiness Church with Signs Following
Believed he'd been ready, nobody knew his pure desire,
The utter sorrow of his repentance for life lived wrong.

The night Dewey, done fighting, came to worship,
Brother Braddock preached on Holy Ghost power.
His words were thunderclaps in the sultry air.

Singing lifted over electric guitar and tambourine,
Excitement so intense even the rattlers felt it,
Striking the top of the box, waiting in the dark.

Brother Braddock, eyes closed, reached into the box,
Pulling out a five-foot diamondback, forearm-thick.
It reposed across his outreached arms as he prayed.

Dewey, swaying, transfixed, took the snake and held it
Above his head, singing in a strange tongue, the rattler
Noising too as it struck him in the neck and Dewey went down.

He refused a doctor, whispering, *Though He slay me,*
Yet will I trust in Him, and the faithful bore him
To Brother Braddock's, where they prayed through the night.

Some said testing God was a sin,
Or if the snake bit you, the Holy Ghost wasn't in you,
But Brother Braddock claimed it was a cleansing.

The means of grace are mysterious,
And the saints an unlikely lot, called out from the world,
Returning as from death, with signs following.

So after three days Dewey stood and walked,
Never again picking up a serpent,
For his heart was whole and his tongue tasted praise.

Revere the Plough

Just before the beans poke up,
You see him out there, evenings,
Walking the field and picking rocks.
"Hard on the plough," he says.
"But most got too much acreage
To fool with it, hopin' they're lucky, I guess."

His old black dog sits at the edge of the field
Watching intently, wondering, maybe, why
A man would hunt something he can't even eat.
But the dog is patient, the man persistent.
This care for tools and tended ground
Gives weight to time in the waning light.

So the elders revered the plough, their lives
Bound to the hammered iron kissing ground.
Many a ploughshare bent and broke
On unforgiving stone, and picking rocks
Was a rite of passage for every child
Born to the land that reared them.

Folks from town will sometimes ask about
That old rusty share rescued from the field
And hanging on the wall of the barn.
"What is it, anyway? What use?"
You smile and unburden their ignorance.
Revive the lost. Revere the plough.

Cattle Magnet

For Keith Wood

Just short of the field, the rake dropped a cotter pin.
He pulled the tractor back around and rummaged
In his pocket. It was late in the day. The sun banged
On the hay, freshly cut and sweetly pungent,
Ready to be turned for baling in the clear September air.
A small metal bar, smooth and bright, lay in his palm,
Its surface stuck with keys and change and all the stuff
That a farmer carries—washers, hog rings, cotter pins.
He chuckled at himself, caught in the act of using
The cattle magnet in such a way. It was a keen device,
Lodging in the cow's first stomach and catching objects
Swallowed in a mouthful of hay. You'd be amazed, he said,
By the magnets recovered at slaughter, holding bits
Of barbed wire, chain, bolts, and nails. There was even
One old boy who found his pocket watch after years of loss.
A farmer loves necessity, inventing what he must in time,
Not presuming to improve the abundant work of God,
But raising mere cleverness to mercy, for Scripture says:
"The righteous man hath regard for the life of his beast."
It is more than metal to metal. This attraction binds us.

Big Cat Story

That spring the cougar killed one of his sheep,
He stayed up all night in the corner of the field
With his .30-30 and a thermos of fortified coffee.
No one had seen big cats in Indiana for many years,
And the warden was doubtful until he saw the tracks.
Then it was all the talk over breakfast at the diner.
"Eggs sunny side up, please—say, did you hear
About that mountain lion over Blue River way?"
North Korea could have launched the Big One
And it wouldn't have mattered more than this.

The night was clear, with a gibbous moon.
He dozed but came awake at the rustle of brush.
He saw movement against the darker woods behind
And marveled as it leapt and cleared
The high fence of the sheepfold, landing lightly,
Though it must have weighed one-fifty or more.
He chambered the rifle and dropped to his knee.
The cat stared straight at him, calm and still,
Tail flicking slightly, eyes the color of moonlight,
Muscles taut and powerful beneath the tawny hide.

His finger rested along the breach but he couldn't move,
Transfixed, held by that disinterested, pitiless gaze.
Then, quite suddenly, the cat bounded back
Over the fence, disappearing into the dark.
He cussed loudly at his loss of will,
Unable to name the mystery that held his hand.
Afterwards he often told how close he had come
To death, himself the hunted, leaving out the part

About not shooting the beast between the eyes
While it stood there, daring him, six feet away.

Indiana Badlands

He wears a hat made of sky
and walks his cougar through the corn.
A buzzard circles overhead.
Now is not the time to ask his name.

A woman watches from the doorway.
She clutches a tiny cameo
and her Bible hides a derringer.
Love will test her vigilance.

It could be midnight. It might be noon.
Time plays every trick it knows
out here. Light moves, they say,
like a ghost across level ground.

The harrowing is hard,
the furrows slaked with tears.
Beware the walking man.
Give solace to the one who waits.

Act of God

When the Mississippi crested at Cairo, Illinois,
they called in the army to blow the levee, sparing the town
and flooding a hundred thousand acres of farmland, doing,
the old Mennonite said, what the military does best,
wreaking havoc in service to the greater good,
a man's livelihood in exchange for a beleaguered city.

He steered the boat over muddy water covering
his ruined crops, dead deer and rabbits floating in the waste.
A barn roof bobbed among the tractor tires
as he neared the homestead built by his grandfather,
now sitting in seven feet of water,
windows blank as a drowned woman's eyes.

People could call it an Act of God if it consoled them,
but building cities on a flood plain or farming the bottom land
were choices made by men. This, in faith, he understood.
He searched the mercury-colored sky for some hint
of sunlight to warm that wide prairie sea. A framed picture
of four generations washed against the bow.

The Dig at Sentry Farm

Skeleton of stillborn
tenderly tucked away   *One foot*
beneath a blanket   *1960*
of soil and tears

Whiskey bottle
pitched out the window   *Two feet*
with a cry of rage   *1920*
the night his wife walked out

Femur of heavy horse
buried where it fell   *Three feet*
beside the furrowed ground   *1870*
pulling hard for twenty years

Musket ball that missed
a deer grazing in sweet grass   *Four feet*
when hungry trappers   *1810*
cut a trail through virgin woods

Shard of broken bowl
left in a fire pit   *Five feet*
as the tribe moved on   *1750*
through winter cold

Beads dropped in haste
by hapless nomad   *Six feet*
running for his life   *1600*
from a nameless beast

Granite tooth of glacier

a million years old   *Seven feet*
jutting through flood plain   *1500*
chewing the lip of time

Running Beans

So little happens on country roads.
Two men walk toward a combine
In the beam of headlights from the pickup
Parked at the edge of a darkened field.
Hell of a thing, how machinery
Always breaks down halfway through
A stand of beans when you're running
Just ahead of cold November rain.

So little happens. They approach
The green dragon humped against the night,
Its great roar silent as they poke around
The header for a clue.   Bruised knuckles
And a few cusses clear the jam and soon
They fire the feisty girl up. Coyotes pause
At the sound and watch the tiny glow
Of cigarettes across the dark.

So little happens. Blue Diamond,
Old Gundy's champion racing pigeon,
Guided by the geomagnetic forces
Coursing in his blood, had paused atop
The combine at dusk on his journey home.
When the big diesel heaves, belching smoke
And shaking the ground for half a mile,
Blue Diamond is airborne, seeking refuge.

The moon, dimming in its last quarter,
Reaches the celestial equator.
The hungry beast moves down the field,
Mysterious innards cutting, threshing,

And cleaning the beans in seconds
As the planet tilts past harvest time.
The ancestors would be amazed.
So much happens on country roads.

Advent

Hawk glares from the fence row by the lane,
Eyes more piercing than feeble winter sun.
Doves scatter from the leafless apple tree,
And a rabbit hugs the brush, hoping for life.
So much depends on how the morning goes.

Old Man Lamb pokes the ground with his stick
As though looking for water in a dry place.
He shudders, says it's angels touching him.
Hawk retreats. The doves find apple seeds.
Rabbit rests. Lamb whistles for a drink.

Winter Tales

For Pat Tempest

On a bright and brittle January day
The neighbor wheels the old Case tractor
Out of his yard and down the narrow road
Past wide snowy fields,
His big black Lab perched in the bucket
Like a navigator on a great white sea.

He's on a voyage of discovery
To see what tales a country road can tell.
Lord knows he'd rather have stories
Than money in the bank, so long as
A good yarn is still worth a cup of coffee.

He waves at old Taylor by the hundred-year oaks,
Who's still raising hogs. No kids of his own—
Lost his privates in the war.
The nephew fed stock and drove the tractor 'til
He blew himself up in the farrowing barn.
They said he was cooking meth.

Down here by the creek was Cassie Drew's
Summer cottage before the fire—for years
The only colored person in these parts.
Folks said she ran a house on the Avenue
In Indianapolis. Brought her working girls out
Every August to spend a few days on their feet.

The boy over there by the big woods
Raises rabbits and keeps to himself.

His wife died young—a saint, they say,
Stubborn and brave as life. Sometimes
He's out there in the field at night just looking up,
Like he still can't believe it. Like he still believes.

They make the turn at Freeport Road.
The dog barks at a deer flashing white under-tail
In the sharp sunlight.
A bottle glints like emerald
In the snow,
Like the jewel nearly lost,
When the purpose of life is to bear witness,
To see clearly in the dead of winter.

Preservation Blues

The old man died without a will,
And was scarcely buried before
His kin, like ferrets in a burlap bag,
Began fighting for the homestead.
It finally went to auction, sold
To some developer knowing
Only acres, nothing of land.

First to go were two black ash
That stood a century in the yard,
Cut down for mulch and firewood.
The barn was razed, and it looked like
Murder when the great beams fell,
Timbers hewn by hand and pegged,
Not nailed, with a craft long gone.

Harder than a headstone, this wood
Outlasted long prairie winters,
Keeping livestock and livery dry
Before it fell to desolation.
An old-school cabinetmaker could take
These planks, cut thick and wide
From ancient native oak, and build
A table worthy of the wood,
A chest to hold memories
Hidden in its grain, scant tribute
To what was lost here after all.

The rural route carrier stopped
One day, remembering,
And saw an ash seedling growing

From a cracked timber in the weeds.
She dragged it to her truck
For safe passage to a better place,
Where old wood could return to soil
And tiny branches touch the sky.

Bail Jumper

Across from the courthouse
The neon signs blink day and night
In shabby offices where bondsmen
Ply their trade, the windows plastered
With pictures of the jumpers—mug shots,
Always awful, made worse by the neon glare,
Cast in a series of seamy crimes—
Possession, prostitution, theft,
The feature of the day being Udell Pinkham—
Grand theft auto and larceny—
Smooth and hard and mostly amoral,
The one you hope your daughter never meets.
Only a bondsman with a license to carry
Would bail him out of jail and he still took off.

Some would call it fate, others, divine justice,
That caused Udell, drinking bourbon in a stolen car,
To stray out of the city onto roads
With names like 200 East and 400 South,
Where he'd have been lost forever
Except he crashed in the neighbor's cornfield.
He stumbled in a daze up to the barn
And tried to hotwire a '68 F-150
Before he felt the cold steel on his neck
And heard the neighbor saying,
"If I wasn't a Christian, I'd blow a hole
In your head, but I'll wait for the sheriff."
The old man trussed Udell like a butchered hog
And let the field hydrant run on his face
Until the county boys arrived to take him in.
From his prison cell, Udell always said

He'd rather face an angry bondsman
Than a farmer with a thirty-ought-six.

Eminent Domain

She learned to sleep through traffic noise
Growing louder on the two-lane into town,
And she ignored the dozers breaking ground
For subdivisions on the next farm over.
She was born in the house before
It had running water and electric lights,
And she remembered her father's first tractor
And his mercy for the old workhorse,
Whom he put out to pasture—not shooting him
When he couldn't pull anymore.

When the interstate came through
And the house was targeted for demolition,
She held them off for three days with a shotgun
Before they lobbed teargas through the window
And two brawny troopers hauled
Her skinny little frame out on a stretcher.
The outrage faded as the county prospered.
Some things stand in the way of progress,
And it's easier just to shoot them
When they can't pull anymore.

Circling Square

Reflections on the Wideman-Gerig Round Barn
(Fulton County, Indiana)

A straight line is a farmer's friend,
the acres cornered and the crop rows
stretched like piano strings between
the road and horizon, where wind
is making music for those who hear.

And into this geometry
of angles comes a barn built round
to ease the labor of long hard days,
with cattle stanchions in a circle,
hay dropping from loft to center.

The roof is most amazing, like
a quilt made out of wood, where arc
and angle, art and engineering,
converge in vaulted space, as grace
and strength unite to brace the barn
against the darkest prairie storms.

And here he may have stood, among
the quiet cows, when light fell through
the cupola glass upon him,
before the war took one more boy
from circle of life to ranks of death.

Almost abandoned after that,
and leaning toward the ground, it could
have burned in a fireman's muster,

but it was rescued, brought to life,
a precious jewel in farming's crown.

The great barn keeps its stories safe,
for scripture says: The Lord will send
a blessing on your barn and all
you do. In this we dare to hope,
and circle back to center again.

Rabbit Rain

Lotus Granger loves rabbit rain,
The light, quick patter barely touching ground,
Shy drops nibbling hands and face.

From the edge of the field he sees his wife
At the window, head haloed by the lamp
As she sits to receive the evening.

He has walked a lifetime in this field,
Where his father's last workhorse lies buried,
And where he hid geodes for luck as a kid.

His wife is in the parlor tatting linen crosses
For the mission field overseas,
Her nimble fingers seeking God.

He too has a mission, here in this field,
Under rabbit rain, for to love a thing truly
Is to make it whole, like a furrow plowed straight.

The moon-colored cat walks the fencerow,
A mole in her mouth. Good, he thinks.
One less varmint in cultivated ground.

He plants a memory now, the grandson
Lost in a barren desert war he can't explain,
Stalked by phantom grief in the deepening dark.

Eighty-five years old. Survived D-Day,
Saw Auschwitz liberated, beat the cancer,
But he never imagined such a thing.

Maybe after all he doubts that a memory
Loved truly is made whole over time,
Yet a tough man's tears can hide in rabbit rain.

This field was meant for the future, to carry
The family seed. A dubious sacrifice
Does not impress an old man kicking dirt.

In the longest hour, after rabbit rain, he watches
Fireflies turn to shooting stars, burning out
Above the orchard in silent benediction.

Farm Hands

Tilling beans at sunset, he stops midfield,
turns off the loud rumbling tractor, and steps
from the cab, with its high technology
and satellite tracking, to hear again
the skittering killdeer and the choir
of peeping frogs among the trees. He lays
his palm on the ground as if to feel
the heartbeat of a vast and hidden life.
His wife is milking in the barn, alone
in good company with cows at rest,
her palm against a pregnant flank to catch
the flutter of a tiny beating heart.
Late at night, too tired to talk, palm to palm
they touch, enjoined, lives rooted in sweet land.

Keeping Light

Walking to the barn this winter evening,
The dogs nosing newly fallen snow,
I move in a darkness that is not dark,
The mercury vapor light a milky glow

That spills across the yard and fades away
To shadow in the murky dark of the moon.
A hundred years ago, the man who walked
This path by lantern's flicker must have known

A total darkness if his light went out
In a sudden spit of prairie wind.
Sheer isolation in such cold
Might have sped his step and cleared his mind.

Tales were told of those who lost their way
In a blizzard from house to barn, found
Too late by searchers after sunrise,
Faces forward, gone to the ground.

If snow should take me so,
May I fall toward light, without a sound,
Welcomed by a field of winter stars,
Eyes of glory, the finest kind.

Kicking the Devil

Listen, Grangers, to the muse
who sings your labor into legend.
There is a mystery here.
The suffering of a righteous man
is like a rain of stones on ripened fruit.

Cornstalks rattled in the wind,
a bereft and restless sound,
and a combine roared across the field,
as back in the yard Kunz ran the auger,
churning golden grain into the dryer.

No ordinary day, he thought,
too warm for autumn. He kicked
loose corn into the chute and slipped.
The auger caught his foot. He heard
the cracking bone before he felt the pain.

Yes, Grangers, he crawled to the truck,
his bloody stump trailing dust,
and used a stick to work the clutch.
That two-mile drive to the hospital
must have gone straight through Hell.

No ordinary day, when a man's life
is measured in pints of blood.
Kunz dreamed he danced in the corn
with the woman he never married.
Regret is not for the weak. He awoke.

He remembered deer foraging

in winter at field edge, senses keen
to a world that took and sometimes gave.
He knew that hunger. *Trit den Teufel*,
his grandmother said. Kick the devil.

So Kunz told the doctors a peg leg
had more use than a phony foot
around the farm. Say now, Grangers,
tell it true, where such endurance comes from,
gathering good harvest from the stones.

The Meaning of Romance

The snow blew lightly over fields and fence-rows
toward the woods that day. The white air
blazed with the blood-red flash of cardinals
darting skyward as they drove the back country
and drank the bliss of a stark and lovely winter afternoon.

From the truck they saw the steer half over the fence,
legs tangled in the wire, unfazed by his predicament
as he munched on hardy winter grass
that grew brown-green in the ditch along the road.
He had seized his moment of bliss and was content.

They stopped at the house and told the neighbor,
who thanked them with a knowing chuckle, saying
he'd go down to the field and see about it,
the weathered stockman finding bliss
in a winter dance with a wayward steer.

Carrying Sea Stones to a Prairie Field

Turn them slowly in your hands,
Cool and hard, made smooth
By the work of ancient tides
And North Atlantic storms.

Read the scroll of rings,
Their faces etched with journeys,
Granite pink and mottled green,
Tortoise shell in moonlight.

Drop them into the furrow,
Shadowed by the beans,
Full of August, undulant,
A quiet inland sea.

Feel dust rising where they fall,
Like spray off the Viking keel
That pushed them ashore,
Shifting land for a time.

See the Penobscot woman
Fishing, amazed by the boat,
Bruising her heel on this one
As she ran to tell the news.

Embrace the life of stones,
The pulse older than your own,
A geography of patience
In which you mark a place.

Say it is not their final rest

As the world remakes itself,
Nor yours when you lie among them
For journeys just beginning.

Tornado Season

I

Salvation Moore stood on his porch and mourned
his barns, blown down by a vagrant twister
that also took the neighbor's house, the sound
still ripping at his ears. Nothing faster
or more furious had ever shaken him.
He wondered why men even worked this land
to see it ravaged so, as if the rim
of chance were the only place to stand.
The world lapses into wild disorder,
though he doubted this was an act of God.
Goodness gets tested past Heaven's border,
he guessed, and made coffee to warm his blood.
The neighbor said he'd like to start over.
"Tomorrow, said Sal. "I'll bring the ladder."

II

Salvation Moore had a reputation.
All he needed to frame hip and valley
on the neighbor's roof was a day of sun,
a speed square, saw, and hammer. He
was up like a cat, the way he crept
along those rafters, until the moment
he fell down, lying still, as though he slept,
and volunteer firemen came and went,
for he refused an ambulance and leaned
against a sycamore drinking bark tea,
his favorite cure, and though his forehead burned
from the fall, he muttered: "I'd sooner be
under this open sky than a short sheet
in some dingy ward with really cold feet."

Dharma Blackbird

You have seduced me, Lord, and I am seduced
(Jeremiah 20:7)
                                    – Carthusian Affirmation

On the world's windowsill,
leeward from the rain,
an iridescent blackbird
peers through the glass.

Her cowl is wet,
the wings of her chasuble
glittering. Her gaze
convicts the casual glance.

Take out the trash, she says,
and plant some flowers too,
and if that tractor rusting
in the yard ever starts again,

do not confuse action
with completion, or desire
with the will to freedom
in this place of shadows, no,

saying yes to the impulse
to pray without ceasing
when rain slides off her wings
into that abyss of light,

and fingers press
the windowpane,

almost touching her
before she disappears,

a rush of wings in flight
alone to the Alone,
the very way,
beyond the glass.

Hiding in the Open

A pair of old boots beside the road
and vagrant spores of skunk and coon
are signs of abundant life
that hides out in the open world.

And vagrant spores of skunk and coon
remind one more of men than beasts,
the abiding stench of casual cruelty,
the feral reek of plunder and doom.

Are signs of abundant life
enough to save the child who dangles
by a finger above the pit? No, say some,
it is too late, except for tears, but faith

that hides out in the open world
may yet redeem the barefoot pilgrim
stumbling on a stone to find
a pair of old boots beside the road.

Trash Hauler

Big Mack tri-axle
Roars down 52 east of 9
November fields
Stripped bare of beans and corn
Bulldog in four point formation
On the hood parting fog
Along the double yellow

350 horse
Full chassis fairings
Bumper air dam
Sweetest ride in refuse
Hauling New Jersey trash
Across the prairie
To unholy burial
At an Indiana landfill

Giant mound looms
Unexpectedly
Out of the flat land
Gears changing at the corner
High torque triple countershaft action
Smoothing out the turn
Barely sloshing black coffee
In white cup on the dash

Stopping at the guard house
Tipping the scales at 20 tons
Time for a smoke
Hey man how you doin'
Me I can't complain

Old lady still lets me in at night
How 'bout this fog
Thick as mud since the State line

Must be the highest point
In the county out here now
Ain't even natural
Still hot at the core I reckon
Ten years fifteen if you're lucky
Before she starts leachin'
Bottom liner ain't worth a crap
A hog farm's got better drainage

Hydraulics groan
Bed tilts high
Steam rising off the load
Dozers backfill
Scattering crows
As Mack eases out
To blacktop and open air
Clean machine running fast and light

Walking the Goats

He will separate the people one from another
as a shepherd separates the sheep from the goats.
                    Matthew 25:32

Cotter, the neighbor by the crossroads,
A big farm boy, cheek full of Redman chew,
Was repairing his fence, pounding holes
In hard dry summer dirt
With a tractor-powered augur
When the driveline seized
And he had to quit, while overnight
The Nubian goats got out and started work
On the flower beds at the next farm over.

Blithe, unruly creatures
Named for his favorite girl singers —
Loretta, Tammy, and Dolly — they were
Born to adventure, outwitting their keeper,
Who had agreed to watch them for a week
A few years ago and the owner never came back.

He was always baffled by the Lord's great tale
In which sheep were those who followed,
While the goats were those who strayed
And fell away to His left hand.
It seemed a bit unfair to goats,
Who were simply wayward, without malice,
Though maybe the Lord had bucks in mind,
Foul and randy and apart from the herd.

As he walked his ladies home

With dahlias hanging from their lips,
His ears burning with the neighbor's rebuke,
He thought he understood what it meant,
That some pay attention, though others
Need a push — a way of speaking, to be sure,
Since even lamb may be mutton,
But whether sheep or goat by outward nature,
The heart should attend to works of mercy.

Cotter pondered all of this and reckoned,
If he had to choose, he'd pick a goat,
For heaven's sake, embracing
Lessons only pluck could teach.
Grease the driveline. Fix the fence.

All My Wives

All my wives love me like I am the last man in the world.
They tell me secrets that make me weak in the knees.

All my wives wear laughter like a crown.
When they smile at me it improves my appearance.

All my wives come home to the big country house
After running around the world all day. I stand at the door.

All my wives love the idea of cooking more than cooking.
They eat the simple fare I fix as though it were a feast.

All my wives stay up late like tomorrow was Sunday.
I fall asleep listening to them poke around the house.

All my wives plant flowers and I pick up the weeds.
It is best for the family that it be this way.

All my wives think I would have been a monk without them.
They give me a new vocation. I have taken final vows.

All my wives love me like I am the best man in the world.
They tell me secrets and I fall to my knees in thanks.

Tenth Street Pastorale

April, wet and cold, surrenders
At the corner of Tenth and Jefferson
To an old mestizo standing at the bus stop
With a grocery bag full of sunshine.
They say he makes the weather,
Some old Indian magic to grace
These tired houses,
New light flashing off dirty windows
When he hums a secret music.

Two skinny straw blond kids wheel past
On bicycles, waving to the woman
From the neighborhood center
Who brought food to their house,
Their mother too proud to ask,
But the neighbor —
Everybody calls her Grandma Jake —
Told the social worker the lights were off
And the cupboard empty since their daddy left.

"Ya'll have a good day," they shout,
The Highland lilt in their voices surviving
That long journey a century ago
Over sea to Appalachia,
And the trek north,
When the mines went dark, settling finally
On the Near Eastside of Indianapolis,
Hill people in urban flats
Still digging for a piece of coal.

Black kids in braids and baggy pants

Are rapping in their the bones,
Talk that sings, swaggering, bold,
A way of saying, "Look, we be alive!"
And Grandma Jake is sweeping up dreams
Off the sidewalk. Keeps them in a jar.
Consults with the old man making weather.
They both agree. It's a good day.
Let's dance. Let's don't quit.

Letter from Camp Morton

At night on Talbott Street, across the years,
We hear their voices like a breeze that blows
Among the stately houses built where once
The barracks stood, their dirt floors turned to slush
In winter by half-frozen tramping feet.
The words are fresh and clear ... *My Dearest Wife:*
Please know I live and breathe, a prisoner here.
Some soldiers kindly gave me blankets, chew,
A Bible, but the guards torment us bad.
They forced a boy of just sixteen to bathe
In snow and ice. They scrubbed him with a broom,
And yesterday he died. What sort of beasts
Are men to send a child into this hell?
We must endure or perish here. Last week
A man was shot for stepping out of line
When roll was called. Such pointless cruelties!
At Christmastime, the townsfolk brought us meat
And pies. Perhaps they heard what horror lurks
In their fair city. I will not forget
Their mercy, though this place be blotted out.
Remember that I love you always, Dear,
And if God wills, I shall come home again.

1943 Martin D-18

Pulled from a beat up case
Handled gently like a woman in your arms
Playing the sweetest music you ever felt

Dreadnought body
Mahogany and spruce
Smooth as sea stone
Ebony finger board worn down
Next to low F
Timbre to make any space
Ring like a deserted stairwell
Or an empty subway tunnel
Hard to lose a song with a sound like this

He sits on the stool in a pool of white light
Picking notes from the ancient flattop
Ragged blue jeans, faded denim shirt
Mother-of-pearl buttons and rolled-up sleeves
Smokes in his pocket
Cowboy boots cracked and worn
From standing too many nights
On the highway in the rain

Songs about cold rivers and rainbow trout
Babies birthed in wagons
Caskets carried home on mail trains
Fast horses, slow blues, easy money
Eyes that take no prisoners
The way hearts are broken without a sound

Music older than words

Elemental as weather
Whisper of wind in the mesas
Before the time of man
The fury of gales howling down
New England mountains
Born of glaciers bruising stone

Spirit of wood
Voice of bone
High on the neck
Low in the throat
One note full of fire

The Ballad of Ernie Hudson

I

This is the ballad of Ernie Hudson, laborer, drifter,
Occasional drunk, who was not above having his soul saved
For a hot meal and a warm place to sleep.
Ernie's metaphysics tended toward survival. Listen.

Ernie Hudson lay awake at four o'clock in the morning,
Stroking his pulse and thinking of the children
He may have fathered but had never met. Oh God,
He said, to have held just one of them in my arms.

His rooming house was crammed between a bar
And the high plateau of the downtown loop,
Its pylons covered with graffiti like the tattooed legs
Of a giant holding up a roller coaster.

Below his window a single weed grew from a jagged vein
In the concrete waste. On its stem a single cricket perched,
Flung from the grille of a Kenworth out of Wichita,
Its tires screaming through the night above Ernie's head.

Who knows? It may have been hauling plutonium
To a missile factory somewhere in the Smokies,
But this it left behind, a cricket singing her life-song
As if to break the heart of the only man who heard.

II

It was August and Ernie wore red earmuffs,
Though to keep from losing the song or to shut out
The sudden racket of the world, he never said.
He held to his solitude like a watchman waiting for a sign.

Rush hour. Ernie picked up cans along a busy bridge
For thirty cents a pound. To his muffled ears the noise of traffic
Sounded like a distant storm. He felt a tug at his shirt. He turned.
A little girl cringed against the rail in a wordless panic.

He gathered her up and scrambled over the side to safety,
Brushing the hair from her face and cooing softly to calm her.
Only then he saw the hysterical woman, the angry faces,
And, as he ran, the explosion of light inside his head.

III

In a locked ward where no one ever comes, Ernie Hudson sits
By a darkened window in his earmuffs. He gazes
On a brilliant meadow full of crickets singing,
Singing for the man who was not above having his soul saved.

Busting Rock

Chuck Berry? 'Course, I remember!
It was 1962. I was doin' a dime
at Terre Haute for racketeering.
Bad place to be in them days
if you was colored. Lotta guards
in the Klan back then.

We heard he was comin' in —
guards, inmates — everybody —
crowdin' the hall to see
the man who invented rock and roll.

Sent down two years
for bringin' in that Apache girl
from Juarez to work his club.
They said she was only 14.
I ain't sayin' it was right what he did,
but I seen a movie of his shows,
and them young girls jumpin' on stage,
rubbin' up against him while he played —
it'd cause a decent man to forget his religion.
But the cops, you know, they was layin' for him —
A famous colored guy with lots of money.
You know the drill — ain't much to say.

I played a few licks myself
and I was amazed at what he did
with that guitar — a '59 Gibson,
double cutaway and fancy humbuckers —
the way he'd play high up the neck,
duck-walkin' across the stage,

layin' down those incredible riffs —
Mabellene, Johnny B. Goode,
Memphis, Tennessee —
you'd have to be stone cold dead
not to know somethin' new was bein' born.
Y'all can have Elvis.
Nobody ever heard or seen
nothin' like this before,
leastwise a white Hoosier boy like me.

They could put him in the slammer,
but he blew open doors
and freed us all
every time he played.

Indiana Jack

This summer night my skin is full
of windows and I leap from each
at once into the shadow grass
and come alive the other side
of knowing how to breathe in prayer.
I'm followed by a rabbit called
Indiana Jack.
The night is full of stars. I pluck
them down like apples, no, I gather all
like polished stones upon a beach
that's curving toward a place we have
not been and yet we know.

                                    And Jack
is talking to the crickets now
about the kinds of clover, though
he much prefers tobacco, fresh,
uncured, awash with dew.

                                    I say
to Jack: When morning comes, when sun
is slanting lazily across
the yard, through, yes, the maple leaves,
we'll sit awhile, untangle all
the prophecies we've heard. I'll put
my tongue to the anvil, my ear
to the ground. There is no turning back.

Old Jack is musing. Your kind, he says,
is strange to me – such song and yet
such pointless cruelty and pain,

such love and still no end of war.
I say to Jack: We are without
excuse. Adore the dream. Beware
the shadow of our bent. And still
the angels move among us. Yes,
says Jack, and flits behind the stars.

Seventh Summer

For Daniel Edward Orr

It was summer and I was seven,
And every day burst open
Like a robin's egg, blue and limpid,
Wondrous, a secret that wouldn't keep.
He called me to his study,
And I sat beside him,
The place of important words.
He put his hand on my shoulder
And told me the awful truth.

The best friend
Of my seventh summer was dead,
Hit by a train while playing on the tracks.
Stunned, I knew nothing of grief,
And my silence was the silence of dismay.

Outside, I groped for the meaning
Of the strange quiet in my father's voice,
Reft of easy music, the sound of Sunday morning,
When I dangled my feet over the pew's edge,
Riffling hymnal pages beside my mother
As I watched him, high in the pulpit,
A point of light in the dim sanctuary.

He would have said he was not the light,
But oil for the light, who bore the mercy
Of Christ in a dusty Plymouth over
Old back roads, where rusty trailers
And tarpaper hovels gave up their secrets

To him when he went inside their hearts.
How I marveled at the gifts he left behind,
Solace to the wretched, peace to the riven.

Later I watched him by the pantry sink,
Scrubbing clay pots for his beloved plants.
Then I saw the tears,
Held back no longer by his utter strength,
And the horror of what had happened
Suddenly gored my summer heart.
We stood together crying, man and boy.

All my life I have felt the rumble of the rails
And the shudder of the trestle, the warmth
Of that sunlit afternoon and the water's rush.
So clear, the sound of the last pebble tossed
And the tiny ripples that it made
Before the locomotive's roar consumed it,
Before the train took another rider,
Before my father showed me
How deeply, quietly, love can grieve.

Tongue Wagging

Brownville Junction, Maine, 1954

Blue snow-suited
Little boy
On a field of white
Blowing kisses
To clatter of boxcars
Pulling south toward spring

Red toy metal shovel
Brimming with snow
Like cotton candy
Like the first temptation
Tongue reaching for a taste
Sticking fast to cold steel

Whimpering panic
Mother's rescue
Warm water
A chastening balm
On stinging alchemy
Of flesh and steel

Learning early
Not to stick out
His tongue too far
Blowing kisses
To the memory of that
Red toy metal shovel

Hermit Edge

He lived in a shack by the pine grove
West of 202 on the Wendell Road
In the Massachusetts woods.
Wood stove. No running water.
Folks told kids to stay clear of him,
Though he kept to himself mostly.
Walked everywhere. Ate most days at the diner,
Stopping at the package store on his way home.
He took the daily paper. Forty-two cents a week.
Gave me fifty cents. Keep the change, kid.
Voice like a rusty drain pipe and a half-way smile,
As if he'd remembered something funny
He couldn't repeat, at least not to a twelve-year-old,
Or anyone, maybe, since he didn't say much.
That time we found a snapping turtle in the ditch
Behind the schoolhouse, he arrived
With a broomstick. The turtle grabbed it,
Holding on hard as he carried it home, saying only
The soup was going to be good.
My father called the shack a hermitage,
Except I thought he said hermit edge,
A name that glided off my tongue
And turned the village drunk into something more,
Alone but not lonely, moving toward a distance
Only he could see, as if the rest of us were blind.
One day he was gone — nobody said where —
Over the hill or over the edge, we never knew,
Passing into village lore like one long dead.
Carrying papers, I stopped at the empty shack,
Pushed open the door, peered into the gloom
Made gray by streaky light. Whisky bottles on the floor.

A '62 calendar with a naked girl. A fishing license.
Open Bible on the table — Ezekiel, Chapter 33.
Unsettled by such abandon, I fled.
Time passed until that summer dusk,
In slipping light, I saw him dancing just beyond
The shack, among the birch and pine,
Those last, best lords of New England,
Drinking to their health, listening to their songs,
Gazing into their greener deeps.
Then I began to understand what none suspected.
He was the watchman, the guardian spirit,
Of this holy place, past all human reckoning.
I marveled then. I wonder still if I can learn his secret,
Daring to dance with trees beyond the hermit edge.

Arrowsmith

A Song of the Massachusetts West — 1960

After the spring snows,
when the dirt road through Wendell woods
opened up again, the family drove
to my uncle's place below Montague Falls,
among tobacco fields, near the Connecticut River,
where his game birds blessed the morning
with an ardent clamor.   He was always
in the workshop early, still in his house shoes,
chewing a briar pipe, the acrid sweetness
of Prince Albert smoke heavy on the air.

He charmed me with his spare Yankee speech,
an easy mix of bookish learning and barracks humor.
He taught me how to soak the cedar log,
splitting long slender shafts from the heartwood,
sighting them down my eye for straightness,
sanding them smooth as my ten-year-old cheeks.
For the fletching, we'd pluck a spangled quill
from one of his fighting cocks —
a felony just to own in six states, he said,
making the arrows more exotic.

By lunchtime, I was steeped in the lore
of the long bow — English archers, Algonquin hunters —
hitting the apple at a hundred yards from horseback,
praying forgiveness of the deer slain
to feed a family.   My aunt, who suffered

both of us at moments such as these,
got after him for putting ideas in my head.
 "If he shoots one of Weatherbee's cows, what then?"
He only shrugged and brought out his fiddle,
playing a Scottish reel before he took a nap.

Late in the day, I went out to the field alone,
picking the best we'd made,
fitting nock to bowstring.
I smiled at the pleasant brush
of feathers along my fingers,
pulling back with all my strength.
The arrow flew from the bow in a perfect arc
over the tree line, across the river, disappearing
in the wild red eye of the setting sun.

History Lesson

Our village was a place where friends were always home,
Hidden in the wooded hills above the Quabbin,
Two hundred years of English, Irish, Scots,
Knowing no tongue or race except our own,
Going the first six grades in a two-room school,
Moving each year to the next row of desks.

Then Araz came from New York City, Armenian,
My father said, dark-skinned, with a strange way
Of talking. He was big, boisterous, totally
Free of malice, though full of urban attitude,
The swagger of one who has seen the world.
His oddness drew me. I liked him right away.

Not the older boys, thugs from over Petersham way.
They taunted him and called him "Nigger Lips,"
Though he traded insults easily and held his own
Until the fascists finally outnumbered him. One day
At school, I found them in the boys' room
Standing over him, his face bloodied and shirt torn.

I was frightened, angry, painfully helpless.
They stood there laughing. It was the only time
I ever wished for a gun. This is how wars begin.
Afterward, his family moved away, driven out,
Repeating once more the story of his people,
Where no village is ever home to my lost friend Araz.

Piano Mover

I remember the time
Junior Button came down
From Pelham Hill with his driver
In that old Impala with bullet holes
And "Live Free or Die" plates.

Junior was big as a round baler,
His eyes like aggie marbles.
He walked with a bull penis cane
And wore a Boston Braves cap
Way back on his curly red hair.

I smelled the Blackjack gum
On his breath when he touched
My head like a preacher,
Only more mysterious, saying,
"Havin' a birthday, ain't ya, son?"

The stairs were steep
With a turn in the middle.
Junior went up slowly, cane tapping,
Head cocked, hands outstretched,
Taking in the space.

He laid hands on the piano,
Playing middle C. The sound
Was like a breeze in the upstairs hall.
If he knew I was there, he didn't say,
But smiled in my direction.

His leather harness tightening,

The upright slid over stairs,
Bucking once, belly full of noise.
He whispered and it floated down
Like a sweetly gentled horse.

Folks said he lost his sight
In the Big One fighting Japanese,
Which goes to show how little
They knew about Junior,
Who loved daylight to move pianos.

Lookout's Log – Fire Tower at Noggin Hill

Black thunderheads since noon.
Smoke west of Quabbin on 202.
Units from six towns.   *Jack Stowell*
Birds with wings on fire falling.   *July 1941*

Fork lightning ripping holes in sky.
Tower hit. Insulators shattered.
Perched like old hen on stool for hours.   *George Bass*
Thought I was a goner.   *August 1946*

Wind 30-40 mph. Cab rocked all night.
Flue on wood stove jammed.
No bread. Son born today.   *Jack Stowell*
Paul Robert after his grandfather.   *September 1946*

Clear blue. Leaves like fire.   *George Bass*
Annie's fifth birthday.   *October 1952*

Full beaver moon. Heavy frost.
Bear tracks by spillway.
Trucks collided on Pelham Hill.
Gasoline fire spread to brush.   *Arlen Wilbur*
500 acres scorched.   *November 1955*

10° below. Snowed three days.
Hunters set fire to shed.
New Zealand on short wave   *Paul Stowell*
Says Merry Christmas.   *December 1959*

Smoke south by southwest. Cook fire.
Wampanoags building birch canoe.   *Annie Bass*
Stayed for lunch. Trout and coffee.   *January 1961*

Ice storm. Power lines down.
Rudd house on South Road burned.
Three units called.   *George Bass*
Annie and Paul up for supper.   *February 1963*

Meteor shower!   *Annie Bass Stowell*
                    March 1964

Early thaw. Winds 10-15.
Hawks nesting on tower.   *Paul Stowell*
Radio chatter. War talk.   *April 1966*

Smoke near Shutesbury.
Wildfire. Jumpers dispatched.   *Arlen Wilbur*
Stowell drafted.   *May 1968*

Paul Robert killed near Quang Tri.
Not on any maps.
Hawks hatched on tower flew.   *Annie Bass Stowell*
A scatter of doves in morning.   *June 1969*

Snook Peterson's Second Wife

The night his first wife died of cancer,
he howled like a wounded animal
and disappeared into the woods
with his fishing rod and rifle.
Folks said he was a goner for sure.
They buried his wife in a pauper's grave.

Old Jane at the maple sugar store
up in the village claims she saw him
two weeks later standing buck naked
in the middle of a stream in October.
After that he came home quietly.
Worked odd jobs. Kept to himself.

Winters he drove the town plow.
Nobody in New England knew more
than Snook about moving snow.
Turned nor'easters into wedding cakes,
lonely beautiful work at two a. m.
January mornings, eyeballs raw.

They met the summer he cut grass
at the Eastern Star. She worked in the kitchen.
He knew she wasn't a Rainbow Girl,
the way she walked, and those cheekbones
her Penobscot grandmother gave her,
high and smooth as the wake of a birch canoe.

In his pickup they sat so close
you couldn't tell who was driving.
Snook tipped a bottle of Moxie

and her long fingers dangled Pall Malls
Through the window cranked an inch.
Folks called it love-smoke.

You could claim it was meant to be
without sounding like an opera.
She didn't keep house or cook,
and Snook said less than Coolidge,
though he bled Republican
and voted for Goldwater. She liked LBJ.

Snook wasn't churched, but she insisted,
so he shaved and took her every week.
When she sat on the center aisle,
her skirt riding up her thigh,
Nobody heard the sermon
but men and angels smiled.

Lefties

In the giddy years after the war,
Before television and Cinerama
Took the place of genuine things,
People returned to the game
As to an old familiar friend,
Making up for lost time,
Reading the holy writ of box scores,
Chanting the plainsong of daily lineups.

My father, the Maine farm boy,
A lefty who taught himself cursive
When the schoolmarm said he couldn't,
Went down to seminary in Boston,
At Gordon on the Fenway,
Just a line drive from the Park,
Where the Sox faithful gathered,
Hoping for miracles on a daily basis.

Across the Fenway,
Old Professor Palmer began his classes
With the Lord's Prayer,
Forgetting the English half-way through,
Finishing in ancient Greek.
It was a culture of deep study,
Not so different from the ball diamond,
Except for the swearing and spitting.

Dad roomed across from Calvin Bernhardt,
Madly brilliant, obsessed with a single idea,
That Jesus was left-handed,
The mystery of the ages hidden

In obscure Greek syllables
That Calvin decoded in his sleep
As Dad and the boys sweated out declensions
In the small hours of damp nights on the Fens.

It was 1948 and the whole town
Was praying for a subway series
After the Braves won pennant
And the Sox were still in the chase.
The boys took Calvin to his first game,
Sitting where they always did, in the cheap seats,
Section 38, upper bleachers, straightaway center.

Top of the ninth, two down,
The count full, Sox leading,
Mel Parnell, a southpaw, leaned in
and placing her in the midst they said to him,
As Birdie Tebbetts flashed him signs behind the plate.
"Teacher, this woman has been caught in the act of adultery."
The runner at first led, dove back, as Parnell glared.
Now in the law Moses commanded us to stone such.
He set, pitched, the ball fouled right.
"What do you say about her?" This they said to test him.
Parnell stooped for the rosin, Calvin intoning, *"Iesous kato kupsas,"*
Jesus bent down and wrote with his finger on the ground.
While Dad and the boys looked at him and grinned,
And as they continued to ask him, he stood up and said to them,
Knowing he was probably the only man on the planet
"Let him who is without sin among you be the first
To connect these acts of holy concentration
to throw a stone at her." And once more he bent down and wrote.
As Parnell threw a third strike, batter caught looking.
The crowd rejoiced, arms upraised in victory.

You could say a game is just a game,
And that Calvin was merely crazy,
But maybe Dad and the boys knew then
What Calvin had always understood,
That life loves a game, the play of grace,
And lefties have a better average.

Looking for Pumpsie Green

BA .246 13 HR   74 RBI

New England back road,
Garage sale sign.
You poke through boxes
For the millionth time,
Musty smell sticking
Like dust to old flannels
After sliding into second.
And there it is, the card you want,
Never worth much except to those who know —
Elijah Pumpsie Green,
Called up in 'fifty-nine by the Red Sox,
Last team to cross the color line.

Switch-hitting infielder,
Five years in the majors,
Numbers not great.
Yet what he endured
To play in the yard at Fenway
Isn't on the back of a trading card.
They called him the last to be first,
Like his biblical namesake,
A dark prophetic force
Among those who resisted change.
The baseball was easy, he said,
The rest was hard.

Lived alone. Ate alone.
And if that wasn't enough,
To face Early Wynn in his first at-bat.

Half of South Boston wanted his head.
The jitters never went away.
That's how the game is played.

Which explains what everyone at the time
Thought was strange,
When he walked off the team bus
Stuck in a traffic jam
In the swelter of August
And disappeared for three days.
He booked a room at the Waldorf
And drank beer, watching news reports
About himself on TV.

If he hadn't been missing,
No one would have missed him.

Changeling

Crocus and daffodil are shocked
By a sudden squall in April.
The robins in the pine are quiet,
Dismayed by snowflakes on their wings.
Human footprints in the snow,
Paired with a line of small deep holes,
Wander the pasture toward the woods
To jump the icy brook and end
Abruptly by a stand of birch,
Where an old crutch is left behind,
And, above, a white crow hovers
In the mottled branches, gazing
Quietly toward the rising moon—
One caught between two worlds,
Whispering how much there is to know,
And how little we understand.

Emmaus Road

For Paul Hopkins

We had sole possession
of eighty miles an hour on the Maine turnpike
in summer's sticky maw when the engine
threw a rod near Scarborough Downs.
Gulls drifted in the hot blue air,
horse sweat hung on the salt sea breeze.

We trudged through pine woods
to the track, noses full of evergreen
and dirt road oil. Found a phone
in the bar, dark and empty
except for a man shooting pool,
missing every shot.

Then we waited by the road
like lost disciples searching traffic
for a sign, seeing only Boston bluebloods
racing north for sun and sex,
weary truckers running south,
rigs heavy with timber.

We sat on a ledge of rock
etched with tracings of other lives,
familiar graffiti, vowels missing—
J LVS K and CLSS 69 RCKS—
like cryptic shorthand of weary scribes,
copying mysteries in forgotten tongues.

One of us fretted the time.

The other found blueberries wild
from the wood. In noon's vast nave,
that meal was the end of longing,
a moment true to itself,
clear of noise and carnage.

And the wind off the sea was
a voice familiar to us,
the breath of holy vowels
unlocking words in a tongue we thought
we knew, until we heard them again
for the very first time.

The Lighthouse Keeper
Advertizes for a Wife

Must carry fifty pounds up winding stairs
And cook well with canned goods.
Must make friendly conversation,
Row hard, bail water,
Cut hair, and work all night as needed.
Some doctoring skills preferred,
Using herbs and sea water.

Must be at ease with herself,
For island life is lived alone,
Though less lonely with a good mate
And work to do when not tending light
Or passing tools to fix the ancient horn
That blows loud as the last trumpet,
Warning boats in fog off Skoggin Rocks.

Must have good penmanship for the log
And writing down what matters.
Must know her Bible,
Especially John the Revelator
When nor'easters swallow the island
And even the gulls take cover,
And all seems lost except true love.

Must know some jokes
And maybe how to dance,
Pretty as a pink sea rose in August,
With a good singing voice,
Quick-witted, slow to anger,
Steady as an osprey in the wind,
An apple tree beside a level sea.

The Bootlegger's Daughter

Some people laughed at the gap in her teeth,
but the sound she made saying ordinary things
was like a sweet penny whistle on May Day
when, of all the boys, she picked me for a kiss.

Her daddy made moonshine among the birches,
moving it by night on milk trucks out of Edenville,
a crass and dangerous life for any man,
though he loved his baby girl like August rain.

One day we sat on the big front porch as
she scissored little paper hearts, and I watched
October breezes lift them from her palm. She smiled,
and I was abashed by the feeling in my throat.

I was a stray she dragged around while her daddy
looked askance. He shrugged in vague reproach
and fired rounds into a rusty car on blocks —
a sound like balloons popping in the January air.

In kite-wind March we raced downhill for the joy of it,
splashing through the snow-melt like thoroughbreds,
alive with the thrill of running. It was then I knew
the love of God, in her, willing one thing.

May Day came around again but she wasn't there,
and rumors slid like hungry snakes across the playground.
I bolted through the woods to find burnt ruins, no sign
of them anywhere, the spring air bitter with smoke.

I collapsed among the birch trees, shuddering

and surprised by grief. No leaf stirred and no bird sang. Awhile I lay, then looked toward clearing sky. In sun I saw, pinned to the milky black-laced bark, a red paper heart.

Dragging the River

It was no place for a tenderfoot.
The winters were cold, the moon
a stark and lonely sentry perched
on the edge of the glacier.

The winters were cold. Men feared
the ghosts of Indian chiefs long dead
who lingered in the churchyard
built against the glacier.

The moon, that lonely sentry,
did not see the child, lost as winter
gripped the earth. For days men searched
the woods and dragged the river.

Rash to name a villain—a tenderfoot
selling tonic from his wagon—
they tried him quick as sheet ice
cracking on the dead gray river.

He was doomed to hang Christmas Day,
but the rope broke twice in the cold
of the moon—an omen, they said,
in the shadow of the glacier.

And suddenly the child appeared,
walking in moccasins by the river,
a crescent moon tattooed on his cheek.
Up the glacier, he said, he saw winter's end.

Hardly a man did not weep. The river

brimmed again with fish and beaver.
His mother married the tenderfoot,
and ghosts in the churchyard rested.

The Prayers of the Monks Withhold God's Judgment from the World

Meditation on Psalm 79—A Song of Exile

Flux of voices in a cascade of praise
Chanting Psalter at two a. m.,
The brio of faith persisting in the dark,
Where children starve and armies battle endlessly
For reasons that will fade from human memory,
And yet these voices cry out for patience.

How long will thy jealousy burn like fire?

Cold wind lurks at the corners of the chapel
Like a thief after coins meant for works of mercy,
And angels in beggars' rags roam
The famished orchard of this world, searching
For hidden sweetness, the solace of love
In a loveless time, forgiveness like a treasure lost.

May thy mercy come quickly to meet us

The monastery dog lifts his leg in new snow,
And hooded brothers trek toward breakfast.
They do not speak of the futility
Of human suffering, how it sticks
Like an iron post in frozen ground,
Indifferent, it seems, to the kicks of prayer.

May the groans of the prisoners come before thee

O do not despair, Lord, of what you have made.

Let Hosea Christ reclaim his bride
From the wretched stink of all that has spoiled.
Remember, please, these acts of contemplation,
The self-immolation, the tuning of pure desire
To the perfect pitch of thy glory and love. Amen.

Eutychus Rising

That first warm night in the heartland,
Spring just a rumor, when open fields are still unplowed,
Asleep in the dream of soil for seed,
Eudie Green sits in his truck by the southeast corner
Of the barn—the only place he can hear WSM 650 AM,
    Nashville,
Playing the pure stuff—Merle Haggard, Ferlin Husky,
    Hank Snow.

He is smoking out there where his wife can't see him,
Feeling the rumble deep underground of coal cars
    crossing the trestle
Over Brandywine Creek a mile away. Every star is clear—
Big Dog, Hunter, Rabbit—just at his fingertips, out of reach,
An odd discovery, always for the very first time.

He remembers how fine the old church looked at Easter
From the choir loft in back, above the heads of the faithful,
Pastor's sermon dragging, the loft warm, the candlelight
    soothing,
And how he dozed, tumbling headlong into the pews below.
It felt like falling upward, stars exploding in his head,
And then the sudden darkness of no remembrance.

He awoke to the cheers and joyful weeping of the church,
As if returning home from a long journey,
Though it seemed just a moment's passing,
But time plays tricks on the soul in flight, time plays
Before the Lord like a wayward child in the starlit dark.

The booming chant of the pastor's voice filled his head

like angel song.
"Son, I've tried to write that sermon all my life, but you
    finished it today!
Praise Jesus!" And the congregation said, "Amen!" And
    Eudie also wept,
Not knowing why exactly, but it felt like praise, yes, it felt
    like rain
In the dry places of his soul. And Eudie raised his hands
As if to pray but he was mute with a laughter
    seeking heaven.

Now the swell of music from the radio reaches to a
    closer sky,
And Eudie feels like he alone is listening as this
    plaintive mix
Of joy and sorrow joins the larger music of the night.
He wonders if the stars are startled by the noise,
    the sound
Of planet earth still alive and still home to Eudie Green.

Selections from Hammers In The Fog (1995)

Hammers in the Fog

The night train wailed and shook the ground. At dawn
A crow flew past old headstones leaning in the com.
Coyotes barked in the woods beyond the marsh, hungry
For my chickens, and it thundered in the morning
Without a kiss of rain. I heard hammers in the fog,
Like someone making weather, a distant urgent sound.
My love was baking bread and singing. The neighbor
Put a shotgun in his mouth and pulled the trigger.
Some days warn us and we are still surprised,
Poorly guarded against the angel of dread.

A Day in the Life of Jack Nebraska

Jack Nebraska wakes up at five in the morning
And makes buttermilk biscuits and sausage gravy.
His cats put their paws in the flour and leave
A secret message on the table that he understands.

He sits on his porch on College Avenue
At ten and drinks coffee from a mason jar.
The cicadas drone as he listens to the baseball scores.
The lilacs are in bloom. He dozes one minute.

Jack Nebraska walks to the corner store at noon
To see Angel Vaquero, veteran of one war and four wives.
He is paralyzed below the waist, but Angel has the gift:
He makes love with his eyes. They trade affectionate lies.

At three he visits his daughter, Rose,
A Muslim convert with a name he can't even say.
"She's still my Rose on account of Christ arose. She ain't
    no Arab."
He is full of mercy for her.

Neighborhood dogs are barking at suppertime
When he bumps into a boy on roller skates
Who lugs a giant radio. The boy cusses
And picks up the pieces. Jack Nebraska smiles at progress.

After a plate of liver and potatoes,
He lights a cheroot and watches the girls
In their summer dresses going by at dusk,
Wishing for a moment he was young. He thinks better of it.

From a storefront across the street,
The wail of voices slain in the Spirit
Pulls desperately at the stars. He strokes his cats
And marvels at the excesses of joy. Jack Nebraska sleeps.

Old Girls

Shuffling along Tenth Street between the food stamp office
And the grocery store, they reminded you of raccoons,
Their wide dark-ringed eyes furtive and watchful,
Two sisters with unlikely names, stealing past sixty.
"Our daddy was in the war. He's never been right since."
His military pension kept them going, mostly,
Until the twenty-fifth of every month. When you visited,
Their crinkling faces hid some deep amusement,
While Cleantha pulled her ear and Jolene clicked her dentures.
"He's asleep," they whispered, sitting close together on the sofa,
Though you never saw past the pale green curtain,
Wondering with weird alarm, if he was really there.
The brown picture on the wall showed a slender doughboy
Grinning timelessly into the space between these two
And the world that waited like a rummage sale.

John Milton Jones

> long is the way
> And hard that out of Hell leads up to light
> *Paradise Lost*

Because his mother died giving birth
Nine months to the day that his father was lost
At the bottom of a shaft on Altoona Ridge

And his grandmother took him wet
From the womb and rocked him into childhood
With a name full of angels and number-two coal

Because she was the first woman
From Altoona Ridge to become a teacher
And to return with the music of the poets in her mouth

And he knew the warble and thunder of English verse
And the sweet creaking of fiddles and the haunting chant
Of gospel hymns before he could say his name

Because his sight was bad and voices stirred
Inside his head like ice crackling in April sun
With the still rush of water underneath

And when a mess of steel hit him in the head
At a smelting plant on the Ohio he became
A child again who could barely write his name

Because ancient voices crowded in
And he drifted through the bus stations and missions
Of the world from Chicago to Indianapolis to Louisville

And scraps of song escaped his mouth
About Eden lost and found and lost again
Bearing a child's simple and awful grief

Because his parents made love before they died
Because of poets and angels
Just because

The White Giraffe

The white giraffe is the last of his kind.
He hides on open ground where no one looks.

The white giraffe sticks out his neck in stormy weather.
He stoops for a portrait in his favorite cafe.

The white giraffe plays poker with the tourists.
His cigarette-holder shakes with laughter.

The white giraffe is not a virgin.
He mourns his lover in the subway near the zoo.

The white giraffe goes to the cinema in spotted pajamas.
He dreams in subtitles and feeds popcorn to the bums.

The white giraffe loves cocktail parties on the lawn.
He whispers fortunes and flirts with the President's wife.

The white giraffe ambushes deportation buses.
He keeps a derringer in his vest.

The white giraffe hides outlaw poets in his villa.
He steals matches from the burners of books.

The white giraffe believes in life before death.
He lets the hummingbirds nest upon his head.

Rabbit Light

Winter days shuffle by in old overcoats.
Secretly the rabbits dance, liberating light.
Renegade dreams are loose.
Keep moving now: pray with eyes open, laughing.

Secretly the rabbits dance, liberating light.
Gray mephitic air is washed by snow.
Keep moving now: pray with eyes open, laughing.
Someone is playing the blues trombone.

Gray mephitic air is washed by snow.
On a steam grate an old man huddles, dog in arms.
Someone is playing the blues trombone.
Lonesome ladies walk like horses on a frozen pond.

On a steam grate an old man huddles, dog in arms.
Freight trains come and go. They do not stay.
Lonesome ladies walk like horses on a frozen pond.
Three men smoke and joke, tending a burning barrel.

Freight trains come and go. They do not stay.
Renegade dreams are loose.
Three men smoke and joke, tending a burning barrel.
Winter days shuffle by in old overcoats.

Cottage Home

In the old neighborhood my friend is dreaming of houses,
Of what they were and what they could become again,
Their mute architecture silenced by a century of decay,
Full of stories aching to be told. On a warm summer night
Near Polk and Dorman, we climb a ladder of shadows, laughing
At a splash of moonlight through the roof, and he is saying
"Here, over here, the cornice needs some help," and suddenly
I recall another story of this house, of Emma Rae, whom I knew
In her distress. That summer, her children and their children,
The hapless followed by the helpless, ate everything she had,
And the old man, who left his leg at the Battle of Verdun,
Lay moaning on a cot in the living room, attacked by flies.
Relief arrived, but not a rescue. Say that Emma Rae endured.
Say humility made her smile. Always. It is enough. And let
The architecture sing, my friend, restore the voice, but leave
The moonlit hole in the roof, that prayers might rise for
    Emma Rae.

Up in the Country

For Forrest Cory

The day the spreader broke, we went to town for parts,
I and my neighbor, a man of furrowed years,
Knowing every mile of corn and beans along the road
Like so many freckles on his arm,
Whether good soil or bad, and how the drainage was.

A new John Deere, tires big as a boxcar, went smoking
Down the field, and we talked about a time
When men worked land with horses, and farming
Hurt worse than falling in love, concluding that,
Unlike a horse, a tractor won't pull for a plug of tobacco.

Then a gang of clouds came over, dumping rain.
Thunder shook us, and he laughed: "The old man's gone,
And the boys've got the potato wagon out again!"
And I laughed too at the picture in his head.
This is how a man survives, talking to the sky.

Good Wood

It was in the forties, baseball's greatest years. The Kid,
The story goes, Ted Williams, made the long trek from Boston,
Following the track of trains that hauled white ash straight
And hard, out of cool northern forests, to southern Indiana,
Where the magic work on wood began at Hillerich and Bradsby,
Maker of bats, the best in the world. The old craftsman said:
Two knots, Teddy, for extra hardness. Imagine sunset
On the Ohio River, Louisville nearing sleep, and among
The shadows a man crawling through piles of lumber looking
For thirty-three ounces of strength and beauty, power for power,
To do what he called the single hardest thing in sport:
Hitting a baseball where you want it to go. Remember
Michelangelo, spurning oxcarts full of mediocre stone
To prowl the quarries around Carrara in search of marble
To match his gift. It is the same. And not for nothing
Was Williams called the Splendid Splinter, born to the wood.

Soybeans

The October air was warm and musky, blowing
Over brown fields, heavy with the fragrance
Of freshly combined beans, the breath of harvest.

He was pulling a truckload onto the scales
At the elevator near the rail siding north of town
When a big Cadillac drove up. A man stepped out,
Wearing a three-piece suit and a gold pinky ring.
The man said he had just invested a hundred grand
In soybeans and wanted to see what they looked like.

The farmer stared at the man and was quiet, reaching
For the tobacco in the rear pocket of his jeans,
Where he wore his only ring, a threadbare circle rubbed
By working cans of dip and long hours on the backside
Of a hundred acre run. He scooped up a handful
Of small white beans, the pearls of the prairie, saying:

Soybeans look like a foot of water on the field in April
When you're ready to plant and can't get in;
Like three kids at the kitchen table
Eating macaroni and cheese five nights in a row;
Or like a broken part on the combine when
Your credit with the implement dealer is nearly tapped.

Soybeans look like prayers bouncing off the ceiling
When prices on the Chicago grain market start to drop;
Or like your old man's tears when you tell him
How much the land might bring for subdivisions.
Soybeans look like the first good night of sleep in weeks
When you unload at the elevator and the kids get Christmas.

He spat a little juice on the tire of the Cadillac,
Laughing despite himself and saying to the man:
Now maybe you can tell me what a hundred grand looks like.

NOTES

Letter from Camp Morton
Camp Morton housed Confederate POWs during the
Civil War. It was located near 19th and Talbott Streets in
Indianapolis. No trace of the camp remains today.

1943 Martin D-18
Martin introduced the so-called "dreadnought" guitar
body shape in 1916, named for HMS Dreadnought, a
battleship of the British navy that revolutionized naval
power. Hence the Martin is a "battleship" of a guitar,
large in body and known for its bass resonance. Martin
dreadnought guitars are also known as "D-size" guitars,
with model numbers such as the D-18.

Busting Rock
Berry was convicted under the Mann Act, which made
it a crime to transport a woman across state lines for
"immoral purposes." Jack Johnson, the prizefighter, was
also convicted under the Mann Act, though his case was
racially motivated. Berry's case involved a minor and was
more serious, but it clearly had racial overtones. Berry
played a 1959 Gibson ES335 electric guitar with a double
cutaway neck and classic humbuckers. It defined the early
rock and roll sound.

Emmaus Road
The Masoretic text of the Hebrew scriptures omitted the
vowels. This ancient scribal shorthand resulted in certain
"lost" meanings over many centuries. The poem plays off
that idea and relates it to the disciples' famous encounter
with the resurrected Christ on the Emmaus Road: "And
beginning with Moses and all the Prophets, he explained
to them what was said in all the Scriptures concerning
himself." (Luke 24:27)